Apatosaurus

by Daniel Cohen

Consultant:
Brent Breithaupt
Director
Geological Museum
University of Wyoming

Bridgestone Books
an imprint of Capstone Press
Mankato, Minnesota

Bridgestone Books are published by Capstone Press
151 Good Counsel Drive, P.O. Box 669, Mankato, Minnesota 56002
http://www.capstone-press.com

Library of Congress Cataloging-in-Publication Data
Cohen, Daniel, 1936–
    Apatosaurus/by Daniel Cohen.
    p. cm.—(The Bridgestone Science Library)
    Includes bibliographical references and index.
    Summary: Discusses the physical characteristics, habitat, food, defenses, and extinction
of this huge plant-eating dinosaur.
    ISBN 0-7368-0616-4
    1. Apatosaurus—Juvenile literature. [1. Apatosaurus. 2. The Bridgestone Science Library.]
    I. Title. II. Series.
QE862.S3 C56 2001
567.913'8—dc21   00-021735

Editorial Credits
Erika Mikkelson, editor; Linda Clavel, cover designer and illustrator; Heidi Schoof and
    Kimberly Danger, photo researchers

Photo Credits
American Museum of Natural History/Ben Blackwell and Denis Finnin, 10
Francois Gohier, cover, 16, 20
James P. Rowan, 12
Kent and Donna Dannen, 8
Visuals Unlimited/Ken Lucas, 4; Steve Strickland, 6; A. J. Copley, 14

1 2 3 4 5 6 06 05 04 03 02 01

Table of Contents

Apatosaurus compared to a
5-foot-tall (1.5-meter-tall) human

Apatosaurus

Apatosaurus (ah-PAT-oh-SORE-us) was one of the largest dinosaurs. It was 70 feet (21 meters) long and weighed 36 tons (33 metric tons). Its name means deceptive reptile. Apatosaurus also is called Brontosaurus (BRON-toh-SORE-us). This word means thunder reptile.

deceptive
misleading or not telling the truth

The World of Apatosaurus

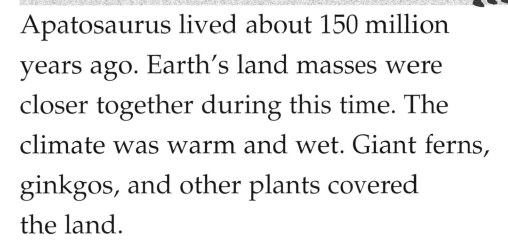

Apatosaurus lived about 150 million years ago. Earth's land masses were closer together during this time. The climate was warm and wet. Giant ferns, ginkgos, and other plants covered the land.

climate
the usual weather in a place

Relatives of Apatosaurus

Apatosaurus belonged to the family of dinosaurs called sauropods (SORE-oh-pods). Sauropods had small heads, long necks, thick bodies, and long tails. Sauropods were the biggest animals ever to walk the earth.

This photo shows a Diplodocus skeleton. Both Apatosaurus and Diplodocus were sauropods.

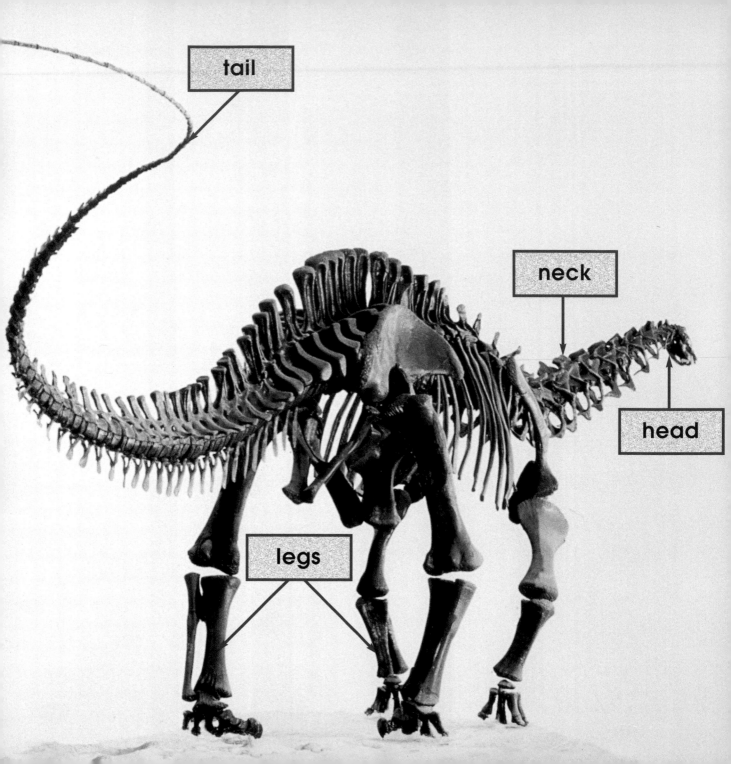

tail

neck

head

legs

Parts of Apatosaurus

Apatosaurus had a small head, long neck, and muscular body. It also had four thick legs and a powerful tail. Apatosaurus often held this long, tapering tail off the ground when it walked. Apatosaurus may have used its tail as a weapon.

taper
to become smaller toward one end

What Apatosaurus Ate

Apatosaurus ate plants. Scientists think Apatosaurus had to eat all day to survive. Its long neck helped it reach leaves on tall trees. Apatosaurus also ate stones. The stones in the dinosaur's stomach helped digest the food.

digest
to break down food so that it can be used by the body

Footprints show that Apatosaurus traveled in groups.

Size as a Defense

An adult Apatosaurus probably was too big for predators to attack. Some scientists think Apatosaurus may have traveled in herds to protect their young from predators.

predator
an animal that hunts and eats other animals for food

The End of Apatosaurus

Apatosaurus and some other giant sauropods became extinct about 140 million years ago. Some sauropods survived another 75 million years after Apatosaurus died out. Scientists are not sure why Apatosaurus and its relatives became extinct.

extinct
no longer living anywhere in the world

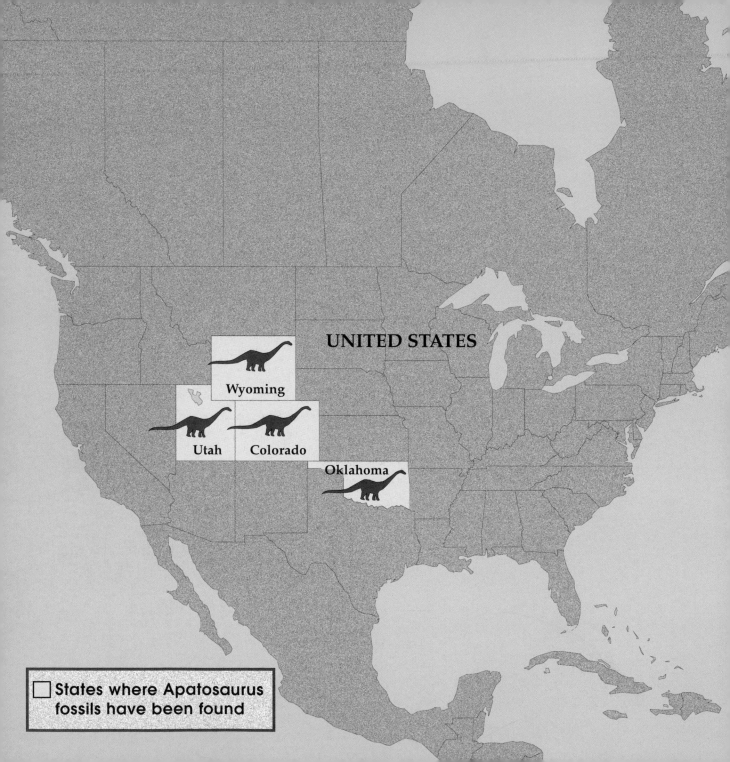

UNITED STATES

Wyoming

Utah   Colorado

Oklahoma

☐ States where Apatosaurus
fossils have been found

Discovering Apatosaurus

Arthur Lakes discovered Apatosaurus fossils in Colorado in 1877. Paleontologist Othniel Charles Marsh named Apatosaurus in 1877. In 1879, Marsh called a dinosaur skeleton found in Wyoming Brontosaurus. Paleontologists later learned that this skeleton was an Apatosaurus.

paleontologist
a scientist who finds and studies fossils

Studying Apatosaurus Today

Paleontologists continue to discover and study fossils of Apatosaurus and its relatives. In 1999, paleontologist J. Michael Parrish used computer models of fossils. He tested how far Apatosaurus could move its neck.

Hands On: The Size of Apatosaurus

Apatosaurus was one of the largest dinosaurs to live in North America. It was 70 feet (21 meters) long from nose to tail. Can you imagine how big this dinosaur was? This activity will show you the size of an Apatosaurus.

What You Need

A large open area
15 to 20 friends
A tape measure
Paper
Pencil

What You Do

1. Have one person lie on the ground.
2. The next person should measure the length of the person from head to toe. Record the length on a piece of paper. This person should then lie down with his or her head touching the other person's feet.
3. The next person should measure the length of the second person and add the lengths of the first two people.
4. Continue to add people until the total length of their bodies is about 70 feet (21 meters). How many people did it take to equal the length of an Apatosaurus? How long was Apatosaurus compared to the size of your school or playground?

Words to Know

dinosaur (DYE-na-sore)—an extinct land reptile; dinosaurs lived on Earth for more than 150 million years.

fossil (FOSS-uhl)—the remains or traces of something that once lived; bones and footprints can be fossils.

gingko (GING-koh)—a tree with green, fan-shaped leaves

paleontologist (PAY-lee-on-TOL-ah-jist)—a scientist who finds and studies fossils

reptile (REP-tile)—a cold-blooded animal with a backbone; scales cover a reptile's body.

sauropod (SORE-oh-pod)—a member of a group of closely related dinosaurs with long necks, thick bodies, and long tails

Read More

Coleman, Graham. *Looking at Apatosaurus/Brontosaurus.* The New Dinosaur Collection. Milwaukee: Gareth Stevens Publishing, 1995.

Landau, Elaine. *Apatosaurus.* A True Book. New York: Children's Press, 1999.

Internet Sites

Kinetosaurs: Dinosaur Database
http://www.childrensmuseum.org/kinetosaur/e.html
University of Wyoming Geological Museum Tour
http://www.uwyo.edu/geomuseum/Tour.htm
Zoom Dinosaurs
http://www.EnchantedLearning.com/subjects/dinosaurs

Index